Platinum
Su Doku

Platinum
Su Doku

150 Fiendish Puzzles

Compiled by Wayne Gould

Collins

An Imprint of HarperCollinsPublishers

NEW YORK POST PLATINUM SU DOKU. Copyright © 2008 by
Puzzles by Pappocom. All rights reserved. Printed in the
United States of America. No part of this book may be used
or reproduced in any manner whatsoever without written
permission except in the case of brief quotations embodied
in critical articles and reviews. For information, address
HarperCollins Publishers, 10 East 53rd Street, New York,
NY 10022.

HarperCollins books may be purchased for educational,
business, or sales promotional use. For information please
write: Special Markets Department, HarperCollins Publishers,
10 East 53rd Street, New York, NY 10022.

FIRST EDITION

ISBN-13: 978-0-06-157321-7

08 09 10 11 12   RRD   10 9 8 7 6 5

Contents

Introduction

Since its launch in *The Times* in November 2004, Su Doku has become one of the most popular features of the paper and an international phenomenon. In a world where time is apparently a precious commodity, it is a testament to the addictive power of the puzzle that so many people can't wait to tackle it on a daily basis and with such intense concentration. *The Times* books, once they appeared in the bestseller lists, haven't budged since, showing their huge popularity with the book-buying public.

In this latest collection from Wayne Gould, you confront the ultimate mental workout with 150 all new Fiendish Su Doku puzzles. Remember, these puzzles require no guesswork: logic will lead you to a single solution.

A valuable tip from Wayne Gould: 'If you are writing too many pencil marks, it means you are not understanding how the puzzle works. You may be relying too much on mechanical procedures, without appreciating the underlying logic. If, in time, you can shake yourself free of written pencil marks, you will see the Su Doku puzzle for what it is—a thing of beauty!'

Puzzles

			4					8
		7	1		6			
	2		8				4	7
		8			5		3	
5								2
	1		3			8		
6	8				1		9	
			9		8	3		
4					3			

2				6			3	
					3			
	9	8				6		7
		3	9				6	
7								3
	5				8	9		
6		7				4	1	
			8					
	4			2				9

			7			6		4
							2	8
					1	7		
		9			7		8	
3			2	5	4			7
	4		6			2		
		7	1					
1	6							
9		3			8			

Fiendish

	3			8				
		1			2	9	7	
		6					8	
		3		4	8			9
			5		9			
4			7	2		6		
	8					1		
	1	7	2			3		
				3			5	

Su Doku

	2						6	
		4	2		3	9		
		8		5		3		
6				2				3
		3	9		8	7		
8				3				4
		7		4		1		
		6	8		1	2		
	1						4	

Fiendish

1			6		5			7
		6	2		7	8		
6	5			9			3	8
3								9
8	9			5			7	2
		4	8		2	3		
7			5		3			1

	5						1	
6				3				5
3		4		1		9		7
			3		9			
		9		4		2		
			6		8			
8		2		5		6		1
5				9				2
	4						8	

Fiendish

	5			4				
1	6				8		3	
3			9					
9	1			5				7
		6				5		
4				7			8	9
					5			8
	4		6				7	3
				8			4	

	5	4		1		9	6	
9			4		7			1
		9		5		2		
			2		3			
		6		7		8		
1			3		5			2
	7	3		8		4	9	

Fiendish

		1		2		6		
				3				
5		6	1		7	4		8
	7		2		8		6	
	2		4		3		9	
4		3	6		9	7		2
				5				
		7		4		5		

Su Doku

		1				2		
	8		3		5		1	
5				7				8
	7		5		2		4	
1								6
	4		1		9		7	
3				5				2
	6		2		8		9	
		7				6		

Fiendish

					7	1		
		2				9		4
	7			6				8
			9					2
7	9						1	6
2					6			
3				2			5	
1		7				6		
		4	5					

Su Doku

9					5		6	
	6		4		8			1
						2		9
						5	9	2
7								3
6	8	5						
5		9						
4			6		7		1	
	7		5					8

Fiendish

		2		3				
		8	9	4			1	
5					2	6		
	5							4
	3						7	
6							2	
		9	6					3
	1			2	4	9		
				8		7		

Su Doku

7	4			3				
2				6				
1		5			4			
	9				2			3
	1		6		3		7	
4			9				8	
			4			3		6
				2				4
				7			2	5

Fiendish

		6		3				7
					5	1		
		5	4					
	2		5			6	1	
	9						7	
	6	3			8		4	
					3	2		
		1	9					
3				1		9		

Su Doku

2					3				8
				8		1			
	5	8					4	3	
	8				9			1	
		9		2		3	8		
	7				4			6	
	2	3					9	4	
				4		5			
6					2				1

Fiendish

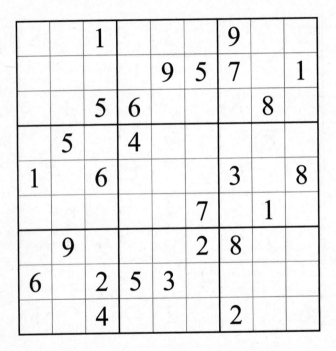

3							5	
	9		3		8			
					4		2	1
	3			2		6		8
1		4		3			7	
4	5		6					
			9		5		8	
	1							2

Fiendish

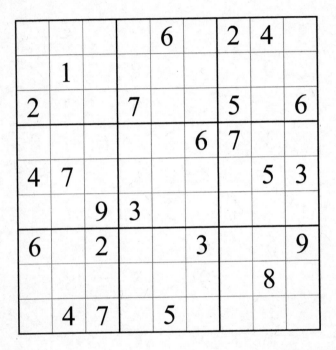

		1	9		8			5
				5				9
	2						3	
			5		3		8	
		3		8		4		
	1		6		9			
	8						2	
3				2				
9			3		4	1		

Fiendish

					5	1	8	
		7		9		3		
		1					6	
			5				1	
4		9				5		2
	7				3			
	1					6		
		2		7		9		
	4	8	6					

5	9						1	
		2			6			
7				3		4		
		4			2			
	5		6		8		2	
			1			6		
		3		2				1
			3			9		
	8						4	5

Fiendish

		3				4		
8	9			1			2	3
7			3		5			6
				4				
		2	8		6	9		
				3				
1			4		7			9
4	3			9			1	7
		7				6		

1	4							
	5		1			2		
		6			9			8
		3						9
			8	9	7			
6						5		
9			5			4		
		8			3		9	
							7	2

Fiendish

7	8		3					
				9				
2				1	6	9	7	
								8
8	4	3				5	9	1
6								
	3	1	5	7				9
				2				
					3		1	7

4						8		7
9	3		7			1		
				3				
	5			9		7		
8		4				5		6
		9		2			1	
				8				
		8			3		4	5
6		5						2

Fiendish

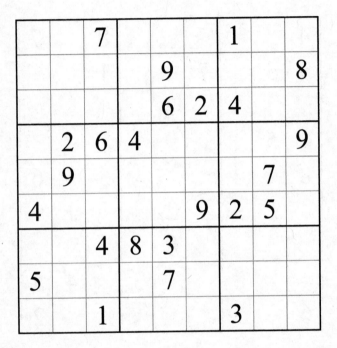

5								3
	8					7	6	
	6		7		8			
		2		4		5		
			5	1	7			
		6		3		9		
			9		1		4	
	7	8					9	
2								7

Fiendish

			1					
	3		9			6	1	
	6	2			4	8		
		1					5	
8				3				7
	2					3		
		7	1			9	3	
	1	8			3		6	
			5					

Su Doku

							5	7
						4		2
		9	1					
	4		9		3	1		
	6		5	8	1		2	
		1	6		2		7	
					6	7		
3		2						
1	5							

Fiendish

					6		5	
5				4	7			
	3	9				4		
	6	3						5
	8			7			6	
2						3	9	
		4				5	7	
			7	6				8
	9		3					

		3	6	1	5	9		
1			8		9			6
				2				
	1						8	
5			9		8			7
	4						9	
				6				
4			1		3			8
		9	7	8	2	5		

Fiendish

	6					3		8
8			4			7		
		3		6				4
					2		5	
1								2
	8		9					
9				5		6		
		5			8			3
3		7					4	

Su Doku

8			3			4		6
		7			6			
3							9	
	8			7				2
			5		2			
9				4			3	
	5							3
			6			7		
7		2			1			5

Fiendish

	7						8	
2		4		5		6		3
		8	4		9	5		
				4				
	8		2		7		6	
				8				
		7	3		2	8		
9		3		1		7		5
	1						9	

Su Doku

		7				8		
			5		1			
	9			3			7	
9	4						5	2
	3			1			6	
8	5						3	1
	6			5			4	
			9		4			
		5				2		

Fiendish

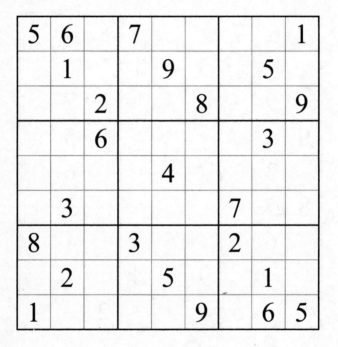

Su Doku

3	6						4	7
			8	6	4			
	3	4	6		7	5	1	
6								4
	2	7	4		9	8	3	
			1	5	2			
9	1						5	3

Fiendish

		7	8					
5	4		7					3
	3				9			
4						7	2	
		5		9		4		
	6	1						8
			2				8	
2					4		3	9
					3	6		

	7							3
1	5	3			6			
					3	6	2	
					7	2		4
				4				
8		9	5					
	1	2	6					
			1			8	4	6
4							1	

Fiendish

		6				9		
	3		5		2		6	
				3				
3	2						8	4
4			6		3			2
6	8						1	9
				4				
	1		9		5		7	
		8				1		

Su Doku

		9		5	2	8		
			9				3	
8			4					
7	6					3		2
	4						5	
9		3					4	6
					1			7
	5				8			
		7	3	2		9		

Fiendish

2	3		5			7		
		7		9		8		
								4
	6		1					
7			4		2			6
					8		4	
3								
		2		3		4		
		9			4		2	1

Su Doku

	6						7	
			4		8		3	
4				1	5	6		
		6				9		
			5	4	3			
		1				4		
		8	3	5				7
	1		6		7			
	7						6	

Fiendish

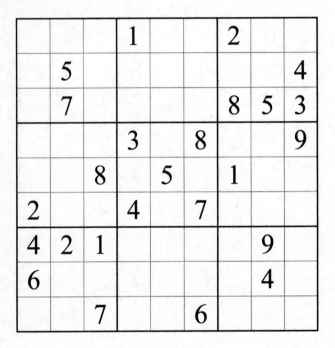

Su Doku

2					9			
				1				
	1	9	2			4		5
1			7			5	6	
			9		6			
	6	5			8			2
7		4			2	6	9	
				9				
			8					3

Fiendish

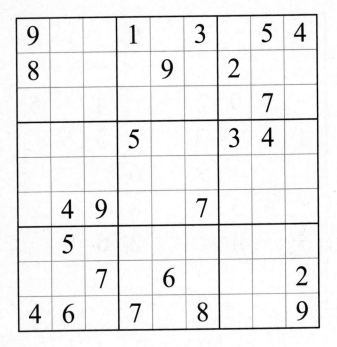

8				1				3
	5						8	
	3	2				5	7	
4			3		7			8
			1		5			
5			9		8			2
	9	4				2	3	
	6						4	
2				5				9

Fiendish

	4	9	5					
			4					5
1		5		7	8			
					2	4		
5	3						9	8
		8	1					
			2	1		8		9
7					4			
					7	3	2	

Su Doku

			7		6		3	
	5	6	2	8				
4					1			
1							8	
	6	3				7	9	
	7							6
			5					4
				6	4	9	2	
	8		3		2			

Fiendish

7								1
			9				7	
		8	4	3				6
		5					3	
3			6	7	4			9
	7					2		
2				1	5	6		
	5				9			
6								2

2			3					
		3					2	1
		4	7	1				
	7	5	4					
8								7
					6	1	9	
			3	8		2		
6	9					8		
				5				9

Fiendish

9				4			7	
4		6	7					
					2	8		9
5		3						
			9		7			
						9		1
3		4	5					
					1	7		5
	7			3				6

Su Doku

	4						1	8
			9				4	
				4	2			
	7		1			3		5
		6		3		1		
1		8			4		9	
			6	5				
	9				8			
8	5						3	

Fiendish

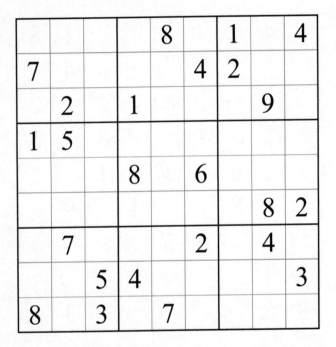

				4				
		8				3		6
1		5	7					
5	9		8					3
		3				8		
6					7		4	5
					1	7		2
4		6				5		
			2					

Fiendish

	1			4	6			
			2				6	1
							5	4
			9	6		8		
9	6						4	5
		5		3	7			
7	8							
4	5				3			
			5	9			7	

Su Doku

	9			3			2	
2								1
		3	6		8	9		
				7				
3	2		9		1		7	8
				5				
		7	5		3	4		
9								7
	8			6			5	

Fiendish

	2						7	
3			6		7			9
		8		4		1		
7			8		4			5
				9				
5			3		1			8
		5		8		3		
2			4		3			6
	9						4	

		8		6		1		
	9			7			3	
			3		2			
	8	3		5		2	9	
7								4
	6	1		2		7	8	
			1		5			
	3			8			1	
		5		3		8		

Fiendish

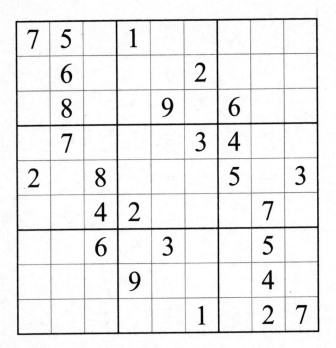

		8	4		1	3		
	1				3			7
				7				6
		1						8
	9		2		6		7	
6						4		
4				5				
2			7				5	
		5	9		4	8		

Fiendish

		6		5		3		9
					3	7		
		2	8					
		1		3	2		6	
5								3
	3		4	9		5		
					5	4		
		5	6					
2		7		4		6		

Su Doku

4					6		1	
	9	1	4					
		8	7			4		
9	7	3						
8								9
						8	6	4
		2			4	1		
					1	3	7	
	1		3					2

Fiendish

	4	7		6				9
	6		2					5
9		3	4					
	8		3		7		2	
					6	9		4
1					2		8	
6				3		7	9	

Su Doku

	1			7				6
				2	9		8	7
9							2	
			5				1	9
4	3				6			
	6							3
5	8		2	4				
2				9			4	

Fiendish

9			5		3		1	
		5		8	1			7
	6					9		1
1	2						4	8
7		9					5	
4			6	7		2		
	7		3		2			4

Su Doku

					6	5		
					9	4		2
1	4		5	2			9	
			3					
	1	9				6	2	
				7				
	6			4	3		8	5
2		4	9					
		1	6					

Fiendish

1						2		
2	9			7			8	6
	7				4	8		
	1		7	8	3		4	
		4	6				1	
4	3			9			5	7
		5						2

Su Doku

7			9	4	6			5
		8				1		
				1				
8	9						7	1
	1		7		3		8	
3	4						5	2
				7				
		6				4		
5			6	3	8			9

Fiendish

6						8	2	
				8	2		6	
			3					
3			6		1		4	
9								7
	7		8		5			3
					4			
	1		9	5				
	3	7						2

	3							
		8	2	7				9
				1	6		2	
		2					4	
	1	4		8		7	6	
	5					3		
	8		9	2				
6				4	1	9		
							7	

			9				3	
4	5			8				
	3	6						7
1						2		6
			6		1			
5		8						4
8						4	1	
				5			8	9
	9				8			

Su Doku

		7						4
6	4				3	2		
		1			7		9	
3	5				1			
			4				6	8
	8		2			7		
		2	9				4	3
7						6		

Fiendish

		3			8		1	
		1	5					
			1			3		4
9		6			2			
	8		4		3		2	
			7			4		8
5		8			1			
					9	1		
	7		3			2		

Su Doku

	3	8	6					7
		9	4		2			
	5							6
	1		5	6				
2								9
				7	3		6	
8							3	
			3		5	9		
5					4	6	1	

Fiendish

				2			4	
		5				1	3	
4	1		8			7		
7			9	8				
				5	2			6
		4			6		2	9
	2	6				3		
	8			1				

Su Doku

	2		1					5
						3		2
		9	4	5				
	7	6					5	8
4	5					6	9	
				6	9	4		
6		8						
1					7		8	

5		1		4				
	9							
	4				7	9		6
7					8			1
		5	2		6	4		
9			7					3
8		2	9				4	
							7	
				5		1		2

Su Doku

		4	6		2	3		8
6				1			4	
							7	
	8			5		1		
			3		9			
		7		4			6	
	5							
	2			9				3
9		3	5		8	7		

Fiendish

	4							6
7				4			9	
9		3	6			2		
					3		7	
3				8				1
	6		9					
		8			5	1		7
	9			7				4
1							2	

			2					6
		2	1				3	
		7		3	9	2	4	
						8	1	
7								5
	6	1						
	3	5	9	8		7		
	8				1	9		
9					3			

Fiendish

	8			9		2	3	
				3				6
6			8					
8		9					7	
1	7						4	2
	2					1		3
					5			7
7				8				
	9	1		6			5	

Su Doku

7		5				2		
8			9		7	1		
	9							
	6				5		8	4
1	2		4				9	
							7	
		7	8		4			6
		3				5		8

Fiendish

2	6		9	7			8	
		5		6				4
		3	4					
			2			8		3
3		9			6			
					5	6		
7				9		1		
	2			1	4		7	9

Su Doku

				7	9		6	2
					8			
4				5		1	9	
3			5			4		
				6				
		6			3			5
	2	9		8				7
			6					
1	8		9	2				

Fiendish

			1			6		
	3				8		2	
6		2		5		3		
	4							5
		5		9		7		
1							6	
		4		7		9		6
	5		3				8	
		7			2			

	7		8					
				6		1		4
6					5	3	2	
		6		1				2
			9		3			
8				2		4		
	5	1	2					8
9		2		8				
					4		5	

Fiendish

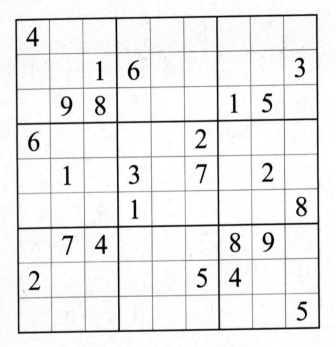

3					7	1	2	
			5					
		4						5
		1		8				4
2			4	3				9
6			1		8			
4					7			
				4				
	9	5	8					1

Fiendish

			6	4	7			
			2				8	5
2			9					
5						7		9
	9						6	
6		1						2
					6			3
1	4				8			
			4	5	3			

						7	9	
	4			6				
6			7	5		1		
3		7			2			
	9						3	
			1			8		9
		8		7	6			4
				9			5	
	2	5						

Fiendish

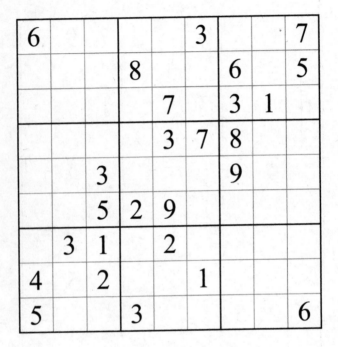

		7				1		
	8			1			5	
			2	8	3			
		5				9		
	7	2	8		9	6	1	
		6				3		
			4	3	6			
	4			5			9	
		8				5		

Fiendish

5			8				9	
		6	2		9			
3	1							
	3	2				4		
			7		6			
		5				1	8	
							3	9
			6		1	8		
	8				5			6

Su Doku

8			1	2	5			
9						3		
			3				5	
		6						1
	3		9		8		7	
1						9		
	1				7			
		8						2
			5	6	3			4

Fiendish

		3					6	
	5			4		8	2	
9					5			4
	6	1			3			
				7				
			6			4	1	
1			9					2
	3	7		8			9	
	2					1		

				1	5		9	4
	9							7
	4	5				8		
			6			3		
2								5
		1			8			
		9				2	3	
8							4	
6	3		5	8				

Fiendish

	4				3	1		
			2	4		9		5
			5			8		
1		6						
9		3				5		2
						6		8
		2			7			
4		5		3	2			
		9	4				8	

Su Doku

		2				4		6
3		5	8			4		6
8	4			1				
1		8						
	7			2			6	
						5		7
				9			4	1
2		6			3	7		8
						3		

Fiendish

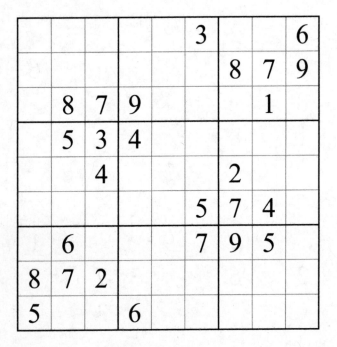

					4		6	3
1		4		3				
								2
9				1			4	
	8		7		3		2	
	7			5				6
2								
				4		8		1
7	4		9					

			6	2			8	
4		7						
				1	4		3	5
	1		5	3				6
9				6	2		7	
6	2		4	5				
						3		9
	3			7	9			

Su Doku

8		2		6		9		
	1		2					7
	4						6	
	6	4	9	3				
				2	4	8	1	
	7						3	
5					2		9	
		3		1		6		8

Fiendish

				9				
		1			6		9	
2			7		1		5	
			5			2	6	
4								3
	7	8			4			
	3		1		8			5
	8		2			6		
				4				

Su Doku

					9	2	5	
	6		2					
	3	1		7		9		
							8	5
	5		6		3		9	
1	4							
		6		8		5	2	
					4		1	
	2	7	1					

Fiendish

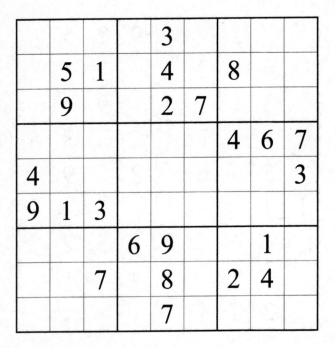

			8	6		4		
				2	9			3
	3						8	
	1	7				3		
5								6
		6				2	7	
	4						1	
6			4	8				
		8		5	1			

Fiendish

3							4	
	2		8	7		6		
		7		1			2	
				4	7			1
2								4
4			3	6				
	9			3		8		
		3		9	6		1	
	5							6

Su Doku

5								7
					5	2	6	
8				4	9	1		
			8					1
	4			7			3	
7					3			
		7	2	8				6
	6	5	4					
4								2

4			2		1	3		5
	5		8					
	6						7	
				8	4		5	
	2						8	
	4		6	1				
	8						1	
					9		4	
1		6	5		8			2

			1					8
	4	6	9					2
						5	9	
		2		4				6
	7		5		8		3	
6				1		9		
	6	8						
3					6	7	1	
7					5			

Fiendish

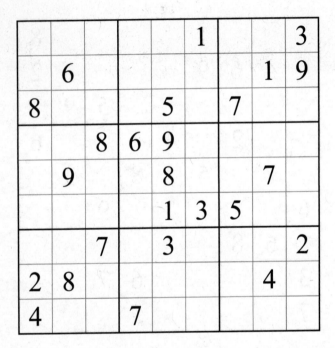

Su Doku

			4		2			9
		8		5	9			3
		2						8
	6				7			
5								4
			9				3	
4						5		
8			2	1		4		
1			8		4			

Fiendish

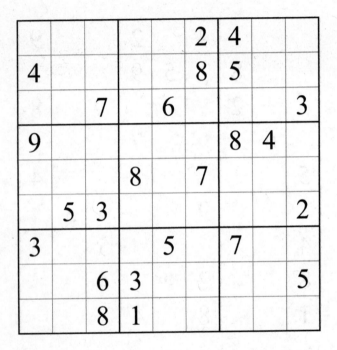

							3	
5					2		9	
			4			2	6	7
				9			2	6
			1		4			
7	6			3				
4	8	2			3			
	3		8					9
	1							

Fiendish

			9				5	
2	4				8			6
8				1	3			7
					5	4		
				9				
		3	6					
6			8	4				3
7			5				2	9
	3				6			

3		5				2		4
	7		1		2		9	
8			9		5			6
		4				8		
6			8		7			2
	3		5		8		2	
1		9				3		7

Fiendish

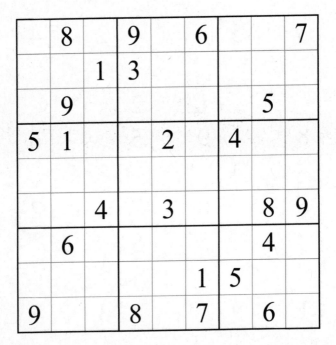

		4					2	
3		1				5		
	6		3	5				
		3	6			8		
	4						9	
		7			4	2		
				7	5		1	
		8				4		9
	5					6		

Fiendish

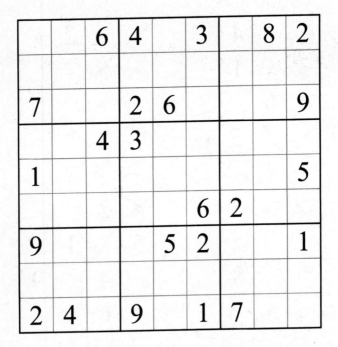

		7	3	2		6		
		1						
4				8	9		1	
7						8		
			7		8			
		5						3
	6		2	4				9
						5		
		8		1	5	2		

Fiendish

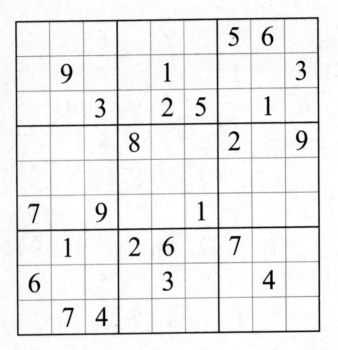

1								3
			5		4			
	2	5				8	4	
5			2		7			4
			6	9	5			
6			8		3			1
	9	3				7	1	
			9		6			
7								2

Fiendish

8						3		
			5			2		9
	4			8	7			
7					6			
	5	8				6	7	
			7					8
			1	4			2	
1		3			9			
		4						5

Su Doku

4			9					2
							8	5
	7			2	5			
1							3	
	4	2	1		7	6	5	
	8							1
			3	7			4	
3	9							
6					2			3

Fiendish

	8	9				5	1	
2								9
	3						2	
		3	5		8	7		
			6		9			
		7	3		2	1		
	9						4	
6								5
	5	8				2	6	

				1	3			8
	7				8			5
	3			9				1
		9			7		2	
		4				5		
	6		2			3		
7				3			4	
5			6				1	
6			9	7				

Fiendish

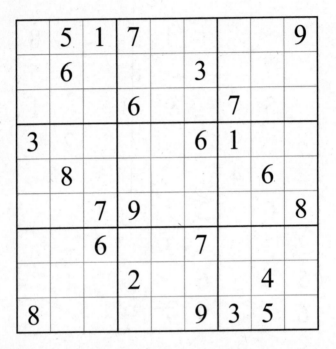

5			7			4		
	7					2		
			8	2		9		
	8	1						6
3								7
4						5	2	
		5		3	6			
		8					5	
		3			7			2

Fiendish

	6						3	8
4			3		9			
		2	6					
					1		6	
3		9				8		1
	2		7					
					6	5		
			5		3			4
2	7						9	

Su Doku

5							9	
					2	3	7	
				8	3			1
		2						
	6	9	3		4	8	2	
						6		
6			9	7				
	3	1	8					
	7							5

Fiendish

		7	4					
	1		6					
9		4					7	8
		1	5					
4		2				3		6
					2	1		
3	7					5		2
					5		9	
					7	6		

6				4		2		
					2		6	4
				1			7	
	8				1	4		2
7		6	9				3	
	9			3				
1	7		5					
		4		8				5

Fiendish

		7		9				1
		2	6		8	7	3	
8	5							
	4	9						
			4		3			
						2	1	
							6	9
	8	3	5		6	4		
7				2		1		

Su Doku

8							1	
	7				6			
			7	3		9		
		3	2			6		
			1	6	4			
		8			5	7		
		1		8	2			
			9				4	
	4							5

Fiendish

				1				3
9			4					
8					6		2	
		6			3	7		
1			5		9			4
		3	2			6		
	1		9					5
					4			9
3				7				

	5		3		4		9	
			1		8			
	4			7			2	
6								2
		7		4		3		
5								8
	2			8			6	
			5		2			
	1		6		3		5	

Fiendish

			4					
1	8			5	9		3	
				6			5	
					2	9		
9		4				6		2
		3	9					
	6			7				
	5		8	1			6	7
					5			

Su Doku

	3				7	2		
	8					1	6	
6			5					
5	9		2				8	1
8	4				1		3	5
					4			3
	6	9					4	
		4	8				1	

Fiendish

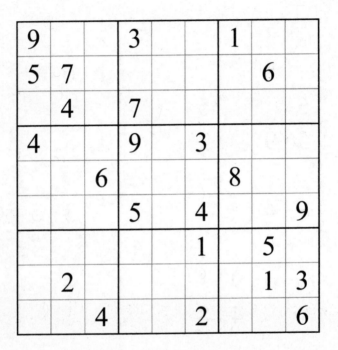

7							2	
			8			3		5
	4	5	9					
		8	4			5		
			6	1	3			
		2			5	6		
					4	9	8	
2		7			8			
	6							1

Fiendish

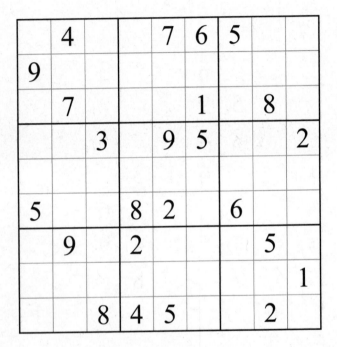

	1					4		
4		6		9	5			
					4	6		
3	4					8	9	
				7				
	2	8					6	3
		4	1					
			2	6		3		7
		2					8	

Fiendish

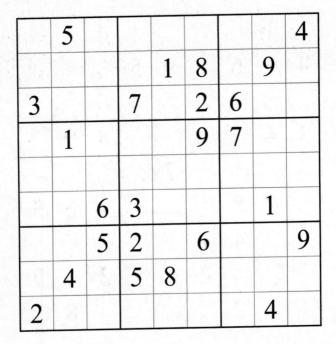

4					2		7	5
	2				8			
1			3	6				
								1
8		3				2		4
9								
				7	3			9
			2				6	
5	7		4					3

Fiendish

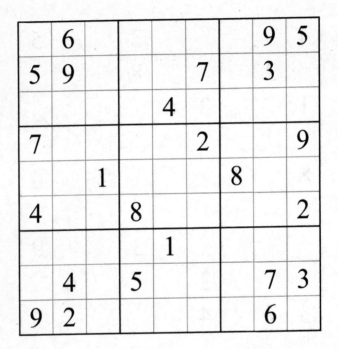

				9			1	
					5	9		
		7		1	3	5		
						4		8
	9	6				3	7	
8		4						
		3	2	7		6		
		1	6					
	4			3				

Fiendish

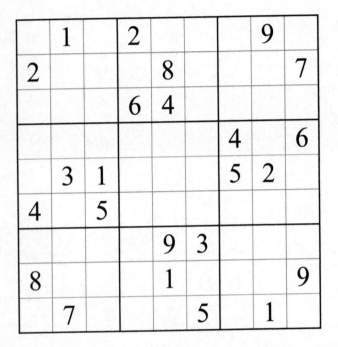

Solutions

1

9	5	6	4	3	7	2	1	8
8	4	7	1	2	6	9	5	3
3	2	1	8	5	9	6	4	7
2	6	8	7	1	5	4	3	9
5	3	9	6	8	4	1	7	2
7	1	4	3	9	2	8	6	5
6	8	3	2	7	1	5	9	4
1	7	5	9	4	8	3	2	6
4	9	2	5	6	3	7	8	1

2

2	7	5	4	6	9	1	3	8
1	6	4	7	8	3	2	9	5
3	9	8	1	5	2	6	4	7
8	2	3	9	7	1	5	6	4
7	1	9	5	4	6	8	2	3
4	5	6	2	3	8	9	7	1
6	8	7	3	9	5	4	1	2
9	3	2	8	1	4	7	5	6
5	4	1	6	2	7	3	8	9

Solutions

8	9	2	7	3	5	6	1	4
5	7	1	9	4	6	3	2	8
4	3	6	8	2	1	7	5	9
6	2	9	3	1	7	4	8	5
3	1	8	2	5	4	9	6	7
7	4	5	6	8	9	2	3	1
2	8	7	1	9	3	5	4	6
1	6	4	5	7	2	8	9	3
9	5	3	4	6	8	1	7	2

7	3	5	9	8	6	2	4	1
8	4	1	3	5	2	9	7	6
9	2	6	4	1	7	5	8	3
6	5	3	1	4	8	7	2	9
1	7	2	5	6	9	8	3	4
4	9	8	7	2	3	6	1	5
3	8	4	6	7	5	1	9	2
5	1	7	2	9	4	3	6	8
2	6	9	8	3	1	4	5	7

Solutions

5

3	2	9	1	8	7	4	6	5
7	5	4	2	6	3	9	8	1
1	6	8	4	5	9	3	7	2
6	7	1	5	2	4	8	9	3
5	4	3	9	1	8	7	2	6
8	9	2	7	3	6	5	1	4
2	8	7	6	4	5	1	3	9
4	3	6	8	9	1	2	5	7
9	1	5	3	7	2	6	4	8

6

1	8	9	6	3	5	2	4	7
4	3	6	2	1	7	8	9	5
2	7	5	4	8	9	6	1	3
6	5	2	7	9	4	1	3	8
3	4	7	1	2	8	5	6	9
8	9	1	3	5	6	4	7	2
5	2	3	9	6	1	7	8	4
9	1	4	8	7	2	3	5	6
7	6	8	5	4	3	9	2	1

Solutions

7

9	5	7	2	8	4	3	1	6
6	2	1	9	3	7	8	4	5
3	8	4	5	1	6	9	2	7
2	6	8	3	7	9	1	5	4
7	3	9	1	4	5	2	6	8
4	1	5	6	2	8	7	9	3
8	9	2	4	5	3	6	7	1
5	7	6	8	9	1	4	3	2
1	4	3	7	6	2	5	8	9

8

8	5	2	7	4	3	1	9	6
1	6	9	5	2	8	7	3	4
3	7	4	9	6	1	8	5	2
9	1	3	8	5	2	4	6	7
7	8	6	3	9	4	5	2	1
4	2	5	1	7	6	3	8	9
2	9	7	4	3	5	6	1	8
5	4	8	6	1	9	2	7	3
6	3	1	2	8	7	9	4	5

Solutions

9

3	5	4	8	1	2	9	6	7
8	1	7	5	9	6	3	2	4
9	6	2	4	3	7	5	8	1
7	3	9	1	5	8	2	4	6
4	8	1	2	6	3	7	5	9
5	2	6	9	7	4	8	1	3
1	9	8	3	4	5	6	7	2
6	4	5	7	2	9	1	3	8
2	7	3	6	8	1	4	9	5

10

7	8	1	5	2	4	6	3	9
2	4	9	8	3	6	1	5	7
5	3	6	1	9	7	4	2	8
9	7	4	2	1	8	3	6	5
3	1	8	9	6	5	2	7	4
6	2	5	4	7	3	8	9	1
4	5	3	6	8	9	7	1	2
8	6	2	7	5	1	9	4	3
1	9	7	3	4	2	5	8	6

Solutions

11

7	3	1	8	9	6	2	5	4
6	8	4	3	2	5	7	1	9
5	9	2	4	7	1	3	6	8
9	7	3	5	6	2	8	4	1
1	5	8	7	4	3	9	2	6
2	4	6	1	8	9	5	7	3
3	1	9	6	5	7	4	8	2
4	6	5	2	3	8	1	9	7
8	2	7	9	1	4	6	3	5

12

4	3	8	2	9	7	1	6	5
5	6	2	1	3	8	9	7	4
9	7	1	4	6	5	2	3	8
8	1	6	9	5	3	7	4	2
7	9	3	8	4	2	5	1	6
2	4	5	7	1	6	8	9	3
3	8	9	6	2	1	4	5	7
1	5	7	3	8	4	6	2	9
6	2	4	5	7	9	3	8	1

Solutions

13

9	3	1	2	7	5	8	6	4
2	6	7	4	9	8	3	5	1
8	5	4	3	6	1	2	7	9
1	4	3	7	8	6	5	9	2
7	9	2	1	5	4	6	8	3
6	8	5	9	2	3	1	4	7
5	1	9	8	4	2	7	3	6
4	2	8	6	3	7	9	1	5
3	7	6	5	1	9	4	2	8

14

1	9	2	8	3	6	4	5	7
7	6	8	9	4	5	3	1	2
5	4	3	1	7	2	6	9	8
9	5	1	2	6	7	8	3	4
2	3	4	5	9	8	1	7	6
6	8	7	4	1	3	5	2	9
8	7	9	6	5	1	2	4	3
3	1	6	7	2	4	9	8	5
4	2	5	3	8	9	7	6	1

Solutions

7	4	6	2	3	8	1	5	9
2	8	9	5	6	1	4	3	7
1	3	5	7	9	4	2	6	8
6	9	7	8	1	2	5	4	3
5	1	8	6	4	3	9	7	2
4	2	3	9	5	7	6	8	1
9	7	2	4	8	5	3	1	6
8	5	1	3	2	6	7	9	4
3	6	4	1	7	9	8	2	5

9	8	6	1	3	2	4	5	7
4	3	7	6	9	5	1	2	8
2	1	5	4	8	7	3	9	6
7	2	8	5	4	9	6	1	3
5	9	4	3	6	1	8	7	2
1	6	3	2	7	8	5	4	9
6	4	9	7	5	3	2	8	1
8	5	1	9	2	6	7	3	4
3	7	2	8	1	4	9	6	5

Solutions

17

2	9	6	7	3	4	1	5	8
7	3	4	8	5	1	6	9	2
1	5	8	9	6	2	4	3	7
4	8	2	6	9	7	5	1	3
5	6	9	2	1	3	8	7	4
3	7	1	5	4	8	2	6	9
8	2	3	1	7	6	9	4	5
9	1	7	4	8	5	3	2	6
6	4	5	3	2	9	7	8	1

18

3	6	1	7	4	8	9	5	2
4	2	8	3	9	5	7	6	1
9	7	5	6	2	1	4	8	3
8	5	7	4	1	3	6	2	9
1	4	6	2	5	9	3	7	8
2	3	9	8	6	7	5	1	4
5	9	3	1	7	2	8	4	6
6	8	2	5	3	4	1	9	7
7	1	4	9	8	6	2	3	5

Solutions

19

3	4	7	2	6	1	8	5	9
2	9	1	3	5	8	7	6	4
5	8	6	7	9	4	3	2	1
9	3	5	1	2	7	6	4	8
8	7	2	5	4	6	9	1	3
1	6	4	8	3	9	2	7	5
4	5	9	6	8	2	1	3	7
7	2	3	9	1	5	4	8	6
6	1	8	4	7	3	5	9	2

20

9	3	5	1	6	8	2	4	7
7	1	6	2	4	5	9	3	8
2	8	4	7	3	9	5	1	6
3	2	8	5	1	6	7	9	4
4	7	1	8	9	2	6	5	3
5	6	9	3	7	4	8	2	1
6	5	2	4	8	3	1	7	9
1	9	3	6	2	7	4	8	5
8	4	7	9	5	1	3	6	2

Solutions

21

7	4	1	9	3	8	2	6	5
8	3	6	4	5	2	7	1	9
5	2	9	1	7	6	8	3	4
4	9	7	5	1	3	6	8	2
6	5	3	2	8	7	4	9	1
2	1	8	6	4	9	5	7	3
1	8	4	7	9	5	3	2	6
3	6	5	8	2	1	9	4	7
9	7	2	3	6	4	1	5	8

22

3	9	4	2	6	5	1	8	7
8	6	7	1	9	4	3	2	5
5	2	1	8	3	7	4	6	9
2	3	6	5	8	9	7	1	4
4	8	9	7	1	6	5	3	2
1	7	5	4	2	3	8	9	6
7	1	3	9	4	2	6	5	8
6	5	2	3	7	8	9	4	1
9	4	8	6	5	1	2	7	3

Solutions

23

5	9	6	8	7	4	2	1	3
4	3	2	5	1	6	7	8	9
7	1	8	2	3	9	4	5	6
1	6	4	7	9	2	5	3	8
3	5	9	6	4	8	1	2	7
8	2	7	1	5	3	6	9	4
9	7	3	4	2	5	8	6	1
6	4	5	3	8	1	9	7	2
2	8	1	9	6	7	3	4	5

24

2	6	3	7	8	9	4	5	1
8	9	5	6	1	4	7	2	3
7	4	1	3	2	5	8	9	6
6	8	9	5	4	1	3	7	2
3	1	2	8	7	6	9	4	5
5	7	4	9	3	2	1	6	8
1	5	8	4	6	7	2	3	9
4	3	6	2	9	8	5	1	7
9	2	7	1	5	3	6	8	4

Solutions

25

1	4	7	3	8	2	9	5	6
8	5	9	1	7	6	2	4	3
2	3	6	4	5	9	7	1	8
7	8	3	6	4	5	1	2	9
5	2	1	8	9	7	3	6	4
6	9	4	2	3	1	5	8	7
9	7	2	5	6	8	4	3	1
4	1	8	7	2	3	6	9	5
3	6	5	9	1	4	8	7	2

26

7	8	9	3	5	2	1	4	6
3	1	6	7	9	4	2	8	5
2	5	4	8	1	6	9	7	3
1	2	5	4	3	9	7	6	8
8	4	3	2	6	7	5	9	1
6	9	7	1	8	5	4	3	2
4	3	1	5	7	8	6	2	9
9	7	8	6	2	1	3	5	4
5	6	2	9	4	3	8	1	7

Solutions

27

4	1	6	9	5	2	8	3	7
9	3	2	7	6	8	1	5	4
5	8	7	4	3	1	2	6	9
3	5	1	6	9	4	7	2	8
8	2	4	3	1	7	5	9	6
7	6	9	8	2	5	4	1	3
2	4	3	5	8	6	9	7	1
1	9	8	2	7	3	6	4	5
6	7	5	1	4	9	3	8	2

28

6	5	7	3	4	8	1	9	2
2	4	3	7	9	1	5	6	8
8	1	9	5	6	2	4	3	7
3	2	6	4	5	7	8	1	9
1	9	5	2	8	3	6	7	4
4	7	8	6	1	9	2	5	3
9	6	4	8	3	5	7	2	1
5	3	2	1	7	4	9	8	6
7	8	1	9	2	6	3	4	5

Solutions

29

5	2	7	4	9	6	1	8	3
9	8	4	1	2	3	7	6	5
1	6	3	7	5	8	4	2	9
3	1	2	6	4	9	5	7	8
8	4	9	5	1	7	2	3	6
7	5	6	8	3	2	9	1	4
6	3	5	9	7	1	8	4	2
4	7	8	2	6	5	3	9	1
2	9	1	3	8	4	6	5	7

30

9	8	4	3	1	6	5	7	2
7	3	5	9	2	8	6	1	4
1	6	2	5	7	4	8	9	3
3	7	1	2	8	9	4	5	6
8	4	9	6	3	5	1	2	7
5	2	6	7	4	1	3	8	9
4	5	7	1	6	2	9	3	8
2	1	8	4	9	3	7	6	5
6	9	3	8	5	7	2	4	1

31

6	1	4	3	2	8	9	5	7
5	8	3	7	6	9	4	1	2
7	2	9	1	5	4	8	6	3
2	4	5	9	7	3	1	8	6
9	6	7	5	8	1	3	2	4
8	3	1	6	4	2	5	7	9
4	9	8	2	1	6	7	3	5
3	7	2	8	9	5	6	4	1
1	5	6	4	3	7	2	9	8

32

1	4	8	9	3	6	2	5	7
5	2	6	1	4	7	8	3	9
7	3	9	5	2	8	4	1	6
4	6	3	2	1	9	7	8	5
9	8	5	4	7	3	1	6	2
2	7	1	6	8	5	3	9	4
6	1	4	8	9	2	5	7	3
3	5	2	7	6	1	9	4	8
8	9	7	3	5	4	6	2	1

Solutions

33

8	7	3	6	1	5	9	4	2
1	2	4	8	3	9	7	5	6
6	9	5	4	2	7	8	3	1
9	1	2	3	7	6	4	8	5
5	3	6	9	4	8	1	2	7
7	4	8	2	5	1	6	9	3
2	8	1	5	6	4	3	7	9
4	5	7	1	9	3	2	6	8
3	6	9	7	8	2	5	1	4

34

2	6	4	5	7	9	3	1	8
8	5	1	4	2	3	7	6	9
7	9	3	8	6	1	5	2	4
4	3	6	1	8	2	9	5	7
1	7	9	6	3	5	4	8	2
5	8	2	9	4	7	1	3	6
9	2	8	3	5	4	6	7	1
6	4	5	7	1	8	2	9	3
3	1	7	2	9	6	8	4	5

Solutions

35

8	1	9	3	2	5	4	7	6
2	4	7	8	9	6	3	5	1
3	6	5	7	1	4	2	9	8
5	8	1	9	7	3	6	4	2
4	7	3	5	6	2	1	8	9
9	2	6	1	4	8	5	3	7
6	5	4	2	8	7	9	1	3
1	3	8	6	5	9	7	2	4
7	9	2	4	3	1	8	6	5

36

5	7	6	1	2	3	9	8	4
2	9	4	7	5	8	6	1	3
1	3	8	4	6	9	5	7	2
7	6	1	9	4	5	2	3	8
4	8	5	2	3	7	1	6	9
3	2	9	6	8	1	4	5	7
6	5	7	3	9	2	8	4	1
9	4	3	8	1	6	7	2	5
8	1	2	5	7	4	3	9	6

Solutions

37

5	1	7	6	4	9	8	2	3
3	2	8	5	7	1	6	9	4
6	9	4	8	3	2	1	7	5
9	4	1	3	8	6	7	5	2
7	3	2	4	1	5	9	6	8
8	5	6	2	9	7	4	3	1
2	6	9	1	5	8	3	4	7
1	7	3	9	2	4	5	8	6
4	8	5	7	6	3	2	1	9

38

5	6	9	7	3	4	8	2	1
7	1	8	2	9	6	4	5	3
3	4	2	5	1	8	6	7	9
9	8	6	1	7	2	5	3	4
2	5	7	9	4	3	1	8	6
4	3	1	6	8	5	7	9	2
8	9	5	3	6	1	2	4	7
6	2	3	4	5	7	9	1	8
1	7	4	8	2	9	3	6	5

Solutions

39

3	6	8	2	9	5	1	4	7
4	5	9	3	7	1	6	8	2
1	7	2	8	6	4	3	9	5
8	3	4	6	2	7	5	1	9
6	9	1	5	8	3	7	2	4
5	2	7	4	1	9	8	3	6
7	4	3	1	5	2	9	6	8
2	8	5	9	3	6	4	7	1
9	1	6	7	4	8	2	5	3

40

9	1	7	8	3	5	2	4	6
5	4	8	7	2	6	9	1	3
6	3	2	1	4	9	8	5	7
4	9	3	6	1	8	7	2	5
8	2	5	3	9	7	4	6	1
7	6	1	4	5	2	3	9	8
3	7	9	2	6	1	5	8	4
2	8	6	5	7	4	1	3	9
1	5	4	9	8	3	6	7	2

Solutions

41

2	7	6	4	1	8	9	5	3
1	5	3	2	9	6	4	7	8
9	8	4	7	5	3	6	2	1
5	3	1	8	6	7	2	9	4
6	2	7	3	4	9	1	8	5
8	4	9	5	2	1	3	6	7
7	1	2	6	8	4	5	3	9
3	9	5	1	7	2	8	4	6
4	6	8	9	3	5	7	1	2

42

8	5	6	4	7	1	9	2	3
1	3	4	5	9	2	8	6	7
9	7	2	8	3	6	5	4	1
3	2	5	7	1	9	6	8	4
4	9	1	6	8	3	7	5	2
6	8	7	2	5	4	3	1	9
7	6	9	1	4	8	2	3	5
2	1	3	9	6	5	4	7	8
5	4	8	3	2	7	1	9	6

Solutions

6	3	9	1	5	2	8	7	4
5	2	4	9	8	7	6	3	1
8	7	1	4	6	3	5	2	9
7	6	5	8	1	4	3	9	2
1	4	2	6	3	9	7	5	8
9	8	3	2	7	5	1	4	6
3	9	8	5	4	1	2	6	7
2	5	6	7	9	8	4	1	3
4	1	7	3	2	6	9	8	5

2	3	8	5	4	1	7	6	9
1	4	7	6	9	3	8	5	2
5	9	6	8	2	7	1	3	4
4	6	5	1	7	9	2	8	3
7	8	3	4	5	2	9	1	6
9	2	1	3	6	8	5	4	7
3	7	4	2	1	5	6	9	8
8	1	2	9	3	6	4	7	5
6	5	9	7	8	4	3	2	1

Solutions

45

8	6	5	2	3	9	1	7	4
1	2	7	4	6	8	5	3	9
4	3	9	7	1	5	6	8	2
3	4	6	1	7	2	9	5	8
9	8	2	5	4	3	7	1	6
7	5	1	8	9	6	4	2	3
6	9	8	3	5	1	2	4	7
2	1	4	6	8	7	3	9	5
5	7	3	9	2	4	8	6	1

46

9	3	4	1	8	5	2	7	6
8	5	6	7	3	2	9	1	4
1	7	2	9	6	4	8	5	3
7	1	5	3	2	8	4	6	9
3	4	8	6	5	9	1	2	7
2	6	9	4	1	7	5	3	8
4	2	1	8	7	3	6	9	5
6	8	3	5	9	1	7	4	2
5	9	7	2	4	6	3	8	1

Solutions

47

2	5	3	4	8	9	7	1	6
4	7	6	3	1	5	9	2	8
8	1	9	2	6	7	4	3	5
1	4	8	7	2	3	5	6	9
3	2	7	9	5	6	1	8	4
9	6	5	1	4	8	3	7	2
7	8	4	5	3	2	6	9	1
5	3	2	6	9	1	8	4	7
6	9	1	8	7	4	2	5	3

48

9	2	6	1	7	3	8	5	4
8	7	5	4	9	6	2	3	1
3	1	4	8	5	2	9	7	6
6	8	2	5	1	9	3	4	7
7	3	1	2	8	4	6	9	5
5	4	9	6	3	7	1	2	8
2	5	8	9	4	1	7	6	3
1	9	7	3	6	5	4	8	2
4	6	3	7	2	8	5	1	9

Solutions

49

8	4	7	5	1	6	9	2	3
9	5	6	7	3	2	1	8	4
1	3	2	8	9	4	5	7	6
4	1	9	3	2	7	6	5	8
6	2	8	1	4	5	3	9	7
5	7	3	9	6	8	4	1	2
7	9	4	6	8	1	2	3	5
3	6	5	2	7	9	8	4	1
2	8	1	4	5	3	7	6	9

50

2	4	9	5	6	1	7	8	3
3	8	7	4	2	9	6	1	5
1	6	5	3	7	8	9	4	2
9	1	6	8	3	2	4	5	7
5	3	2	7	4	6	1	9	8
4	7	8	1	9	5	2	3	6
6	5	4	2	1	3	8	7	9
7	2	3	9	8	4	5	6	1
8	9	1	6	5	7	3	2	4

Solutions

51

2	9	1	7	4	6	5	3	8
7	5	6	2	8	3	4	1	9
4	3	8	9	5	1	6	7	2
1	4	2	6	7	9	3	8	5
8	6	3	4	2	5	7	9	1
9	7	5	1	3	8	2	4	6
3	2	9	5	1	7	8	6	4
5	1	7	8	6	4	9	2	3
6	8	4	3	9	2	1	5	7

52

7	9	3	5	2	6	8	4	1
4	2	6	9	8	1	3	7	5
5	1	8	4	3	7	9	2	6
1	6	5	8	9	2	7	3	4
3	8	2	6	7	4	1	5	9
9	7	4	1	5	3	2	6	8
2	4	9	3	1	5	6	8	7
8	5	7	2	6	9	4	1	3
6	3	1	7	4	8	5	9	2

Solutions

53

2	1	6	3	8	9	5	7	4
7	8	3	6	5	4	9	2	1
9	5	4	7	1	2	3	6	8
1	7	5	4	9	3	6	8	2
8	6	9	5	2	1	4	3	7
4	3	2	8	7	6	1	9	5
5	4	7	9	3	8	2	1	6
6	9	1	2	4	7	8	5	3
3	2	8	1	6	5	7	4	9

54

9	8	2	1	4	5	6	7	3
4	3	6	7	9	8	5	1	2
7	5	1	3	6	2	8	4	9
5	9	3	6	1	4	2	8	7
2	1	8	9	5	7	3	6	4
6	4	7	2	8	3	9	5	1
3	2	4	5	7	6	1	9	8
8	6	9	4	2	1	7	3	5
1	7	5	8	3	9	4	2	6

55

2	4	7	3	6	5	9	1	8
3	6	5	9	8	1	7	4	2
9	8	1	7	4	2	5	6	3
4	7	9	1	2	6	3	8	5
5	2	6	8	3	9	1	7	4
1	3	8	5	7	4	2	9	6
7	1	4	6	5	3	8	2	9
6	9	3	2	1	8	4	5	7
8	5	2	4	9	7	6	3	1

56

5	9	6	2	8	7	1	3	4
7	8	1	9	3	4	2	5	6
3	2	4	1	6	5	7	9	8
1	5	8	7	2	3	4	6	9
9	3	2	8	4	6	5	1	7
4	6	7	5	1	9	3	8	2
6	7	9	3	5	2	8	4	1
2	1	5	4	9	8	6	7	3
8	4	3	6	7	1	9	2	5

Solutions

9	3	2	6	4	5	1	8	7
7	4	8	1	9	2	3	5	6
1	6	5	7	8	3	4	2	9
5	9	4	8	1	6	2	7	3
2	7	3	9	5	4	8	6	1
6	8	1	2	3	7	9	4	5
8	5	9	4	6	1	7	3	2
4	2	6	3	7	9	5	1	8
3	1	7	5	2	8	6	9	4

5	1	2	7	4	6	9	8	3
3	9	4	2	5	8	7	6	1
6	7	8	3	1	9	2	5	4
1	4	3	9	6	5	8	2	7
9	6	7	1	8	2	3	4	5
8	2	5	4	3	7	1	9	6
7	8	1	6	2	4	5	3	9
4	5	9	8	7	3	6	1	2
2	3	6	5	9	1	4	7	8

Solutions

5	9	4	1	3	7	8	2	6
2	6	8	4	9	5	7	3	1
1	7	3	6	2	8	9	4	5
8	5	9	3	7	6	2	1	4
3	2	6	9	4	1	5	7	8
7	4	1	8	5	2	3	6	9
6	1	7	5	8	3	4	9	2
9	3	5	2	1	4	6	8	7
4	8	2	7	6	9	1	5	3

9	2	1	5	3	8	6	7	4
3	5	4	6	1	7	2	8	9
6	7	8	9	4	2	1	5	3
7	3	2	8	6	4	9	1	5
1	8	6	7	9	5	4	3	2
5	4	9	3	2	1	7	6	8
4	6	5	1	8	9	3	2	7
2	1	7	4	5	3	8	9	6
8	9	3	2	7	6	5	4	1

Solutions

61

3	2	8	5	6	9	1	4	7
5	9	4	8	7	1	6	3	2
6	1	7	3	4	2	9	5	8
4	8	3	6	5	7	2	9	1
7	5	2	9	1	8	3	6	4
9	6	1	4	2	3	7	8	5
8	7	6	1	9	5	4	2	3
2	3	9	7	8	4	5	1	6
1	4	5	2	3	6	8	7	9

62

7	5	3	1	4	6	2	8	9
9	6	1	5	8	2	7	3	4
4	8	2	3	9	7	6	1	5
6	7	5	8	1	3	4	9	2
2	1	8	4	7	9	5	6	3
3	9	4	2	6	5	8	7	1
1	2	6	7	3	4	9	5	8
5	3	7	9	2	8	1	4	6
8	4	9	6	5	1	3	2	7

63

7	6	8	4	2	1	3	9	5
9	1	4	5	6	3	2	8	7
3	5	2	8	7	9	1	4	6
5	4	1	3	9	7	6	2	8
8	9	3	2	4	6	5	7	1
6	2	7	1	8	5	4	3	9
4	8	9	6	5	2	7	1	3
2	3	6	7	1	8	9	5	4
1	7	5	9	3	4	8	6	2

64

1	7	6	2	5	4	3	8	9
4	8	9	1	6	3	7	5	2
3	5	2	8	7	9	1	4	6
7	9	1	5	3	2	8	6	4
5	2	4	7	8	6	9	1	3
6	3	8	4	9	1	5	2	7
8	6	3	9	2	5	4	7	1
9	4	5	6	1	7	2	3	8
2	1	7	3	4	8	6	9	5

Solutions

65

4	5	7	8	2	6	9	1	3
2	9	1	4	3	5	6	8	7
3	6	8	7	1	9	4	2	5
9	7	3	6	4	8	2	5	1
8	4	6	1	5	2	7	3	9
1	2	5	9	7	3	8	6	4
7	3	2	5	6	4	1	9	8
5	8	4	2	9	1	3	7	6
6	1	9	3	8	7	5	4	2

66

3	4	7	5	6	8	2	1	9
5	9	2	7	1	3	6	4	8
8	6	1	2	4	9	3	7	5
9	1	3	4	2	5	8	6	7
4	8	6	3	9	7	5	2	1
7	2	5	1	8	6	9	3	4
1	7	9	6	5	2	4	8	3
2	3	8	9	7	4	1	5	6
6	5	4	8	3	1	7	9	2

Solutions

67

8	1	2	4	7	5	9	3	6
3	5	6	1	2	9	4	8	7
9	4	7	3	6	8	1	2	5
7	2	8	5	3	4	6	1	9
6	9	1	7	8	2	3	5	4
4	3	5	9	1	6	8	7	2
1	6	4	8	5	7	2	9	3
5	8	9	2	4	3	7	6	1
2	7	3	6	9	1	5	4	8

68

9	4	7	5	2	3	8	1	6
6	3	5	9	8	1	4	2	7
2	1	8	4	6	7	5	3	9
5	6	4	2	3	8	9	7	1
1	2	3	7	9	5	6	4	8
7	8	9	1	4	6	3	5	2
3	9	2	8	1	4	7	6	5
4	5	1	6	7	9	2	8	3
8	7	6	3	5	2	1	9	4

Solutions

7	9	2	4	3	6	5	1	8
5	8	3	7	1	9	4	6	2
1	4	6	5	2	8	7	9	3
4	7	8	3	6	2	9	5	1
3	1	9	8	5	4	6	2	7
6	2	5	1	9	7	8	3	4
9	6	7	2	4	3	1	8	5
2	5	4	9	8	1	3	7	6
8	3	1	6	7	5	2	4	9

1	5	6	9	3	8	2	7	4
2	9	3	4	7	1	5	8	6
8	4	7	5	6	2	3	9	1
6	7	9	1	5	4	8	2	3
5	1	2	7	8	3	6	4	9
3	8	4	6	2	9	7	1	5
7	2	1	3	4	5	9	6	8
4	3	8	2	9	6	1	5	7
9	6	5	8	1	7	4	3	2

Solutions

7	3	1	9	4	6	8	2	5
4	5	8	3	2	7	1	9	6
2	6	9	8	1	5	7	4	3
8	9	5	2	6	4	3	7	1
6	1	2	7	5	3	9	8	4
3	4	7	1	8	9	6	5	2
9	2	3	4	7	1	5	6	8
1	8	6	5	9	2	4	3	7
5	7	4	6	3	8	2	1	9

6	5	3	7	1	9	8	2	4
7	4	9	5	8	2	3	6	1
1	2	8	3	4	6	7	9	5
3	8	5	6	7	1	2	4	9
9	6	1	4	2	3	5	8	7
2	7	4	8	9	5	6	1	3
5	9	6	2	3	4	1	7	8
8	1	2	9	5	7	4	3	6
4	3	7	1	6	8	9	5	2

Solutions

73

2	3	6	8	9	4	1	5	7
1	4	8	2	7	5	6	3	9
5	7	9	3	1	6	8	2	4
9	6	2	1	3	7	5	4	8
3	1	4	5	8	9	7	6	2
8	5	7	4	6	2	3	9	1
7	8	5	9	2	3	4	1	6
6	2	3	7	4	1	9	8	5
4	9	1	6	5	8	2	7	3

74

2	8	7	9	6	4	5	3	1
4	5	1	7	8	3	9	6	2
9	3	6	5	1	2	8	4	7
1	4	3	8	7	5	2	9	6
7	2	9	6	4	1	3	5	8
5	6	8	3	2	9	1	7	4
8	7	5	2	9	6	4	1	3
3	1	2	4	5	7	6	8	9
6	9	4	1	3	8	7	2	5

9	3	7	1	6	2	8	5	4
6	4	8	5	9	3	2	7	1
5	2	1	8	4	7	3	9	6
3	5	4	6	8	1	9	2	7
8	1	6	7	2	9	4	3	5
2	7	9	4	3	5	1	6	8
4	8	3	2	5	6	7	1	9
1	6	2	9	7	8	5	4	3
7	9	5	3	1	4	6	8	2

6	5	3	9	4	8	7	1	2
4	2	1	5	3	7	8	6	9
8	9	7	1	2	6	3	5	4
9	4	6	8	1	2	5	3	7
7	8	5	4	9	3	6	2	1
3	1	2	7	6	5	4	9	8
5	6	8	2	7	1	9	4	3
2	3	4	6	8	9	1	7	5
1	7	9	3	5	4	2	8	6

Solutions

77

4	3	8	6	9	1	2	5	7
6	7	9	4	5	2	1	8	3
1	5	2	8	3	7	4	9	6
3	1	7	5	6	9	8	2	4
2	6	5	1	4	8	3	7	9
9	8	4	2	7	3	5	6	1
8	4	1	9	2	6	7	3	5
7	2	6	3	1	5	9	4	8
5	9	3	7	8	4	6	1	2

78

6	7	8	1	2	3	9	4	5
2	9	5	4	6	7	1	3	8
4	1	3	8	9	5	7	6	2
7	6	2	9	8	4	5	1	3
5	4	9	6	3	1	2	8	7
8	3	1	7	5	2	4	9	6
1	5	4	3	7	6	8	2	9
9	2	6	5	4	8	3	7	1
3	8	7	2	1	9	6	5	4

Solutions

79

7	2	4	1	8	3	9	6	5
8	1	5	7	9	6	3	4	2
3	6	9	4	5	2	8	1	7
2	7	6	9	3	4	1	5	8
9	8	3	6	1	5	2	7	4
4	5	1	2	7	8	6	9	3
5	3	7	8	6	9	4	2	1
6	4	8	5	2	1	7	3	9
1	9	2	3	4	7	5	8	6

80

5	6	1	3	4	9	7	2	8
2	9	7	6	8	1	3	5	4
3	4	8	5	2	7	9	1	6
7	2	6	4	3	8	5	9	1
1	3	5	2	9	6	4	8	7
9	8	4	7	1	5	2	6	3
8	1	2	9	7	3	6	4	5
4	5	3	1	6	2	8	7	9
6	7	9	8	5	4	1	3	2

Solutions

81

5	9	4	6	7	2	3	1	8
6	7	8	9	1	3	2	4	5
3	1	2	4	8	5	9	7	6
4	8	9	7	5	6	1	3	2
1	6	5	3	2	9	4	8	7
2	3	7	8	4	1	5	6	9
8	5	1	2	3	7	6	9	4
7	2	6	1	9	4	8	5	3
9	4	3	5	6	8	7	2	1

82

8	4	2	3	5	9	7	1	6
7	1	6	2	4	8	3	9	5
9	5	3	6	1	7	2	4	8
4	8	1	5	6	3	9	7	2
3	2	9	7	8	4	6	5	1
5	6	7	9	2	1	4	8	3
2	3	8	4	9	5	1	6	7
6	9	5	1	7	2	8	3	4
1	7	4	8	3	6	5	2	9

Solutions

83

3	4	8	2	5	7	1	9	6
6	9	2	1	4	8	5	3	7
5	1	7	6	3	9	2	4	8
4	5	3	7	6	2	8	1	9
7	2	9	8	1	4	3	6	5
8	6	1	3	9	5	4	7	2
1	3	5	9	8	6	7	2	4
2	8	6	4	7	1	9	5	3
9	7	4	5	2	3	6	8	1

84

5	8	7	1	9	6	2	3	4
9	1	2	5	3	4	7	8	6
6	4	3	8	2	7	5	1	9
8	3	9	2	4	1	6	7	5
1	7	6	3	5	9	8	4	2
4	2	5	6	7	8	1	9	3
3	6	8	4	1	5	9	2	7
7	5	4	9	8	2	3	6	1
2	9	1	7	6	3	4	5	8

Solutions

85

7	3	5	6	8	1	2	4	9
8	4	2	9	5	7	1	6	3
6	9	1	2	4	3	8	5	7
3	6	9	1	2	5	7	8	4
5	7	4	3	9	8	6	1	2
1	2	8	4	7	6	3	9	5
9	8	6	5	3	2	4	7	1
2	5	7	8	1	4	9	3	6
4	1	3	7	6	9	5	2	8

86

2	6	4	9	7	3	5	8	1
1	9	5	8	6	2	7	3	4
8	7	3	4	5	1	2	9	6
6	5	7	2	4	9	8	1	3
4	8	2	1	3	7	9	6	5
3	1	9	5	8	6	4	2	7
9	3	1	7	2	5	6	4	8
7	4	6	3	9	8	1	5	2
5	2	8	6	1	4	3	7	9

Solutions

87

8	5	1	4	7	9	3	6	2
9	6	2	1	3	8	7	5	4
4	3	7	2	5	6	1	9	8
3	7	8	5	9	1	4	2	6
5	9	4	7	6	2	8	3	1
2	1	6	8	4	3	9	7	5
6	2	9	3	8	4	5	1	7
7	4	3	6	1	5	2	8	9
1	8	5	9	2	7	6	4	3

88

4	7	8	1	2	3	6	5	9
5	3	9	7	6	8	1	2	4
6	1	2	4	5	9	3	7	8
7	4	6	2	3	1	8	9	5
2	8	5	6	9	4	7	3	1
1	9	3	5	8	7	4	6	2
3	2	4	8	7	5	9	1	6
9	5	1	3	4	6	2	8	7
8	6	7	9	1	2	5	4	3

Solutions

89

1	7	4	8	3	2	5	6	9
2	3	5	7	6	9	1	8	4
6	8	9	1	4	5	3	2	7
5	9	6	4	1	8	7	3	2
4	2	7	9	5	3	8	1	6
8	1	3	6	2	7	4	9	5
3	5	1	2	7	6	9	4	8
9	4	2	5	8	1	6	7	3
7	6	8	3	9	4	2	5	1

90

4	5	6	9	3	1	7	8	2
7	2	1	6	5	8	9	4	3
3	9	8	7	2	4	1	5	6
6	4	7	5	8	2	3	1	9
8	1	5	3	9	7	6	2	4
9	3	2	1	4	6	5	7	8
5	7	4	2	6	3	8	9	1
2	6	9	8	1	5	4	3	7
1	8	3	4	7	9	2	6	5

Solutions

91

3	5	8	9	4	7	1	2	6
9	6	2	5	8	1	3	4	7
1	7	4	3	2	6	9	8	5
5	3	1	2	9	8	6	7	4
2	8	7	4	6	3	5	1	9
6	4	9	1	7	5	8	3	2
4	2	3	6	1	9	7	5	8
8	1	6	7	5	4	2	9	3
7	9	5	8	3	2	4	6	1

92

3	5	8	6	4	7	2	9	1
9	7	4	2	3	1	6	8	5
2	1	6	9	8	5	3	7	4
5	3	2	8	6	4	7	1	9
4	9	7	3	1	2	5	6	8
6	8	1	5	7	9	4	3	2
7	2	5	1	9	6	8	4	3
1	4	3	7	2	8	9	5	6
8	6	9	4	5	3	1	2	7

Solutions

93

5	1	3	8	2	4	7	9	6
7	4	9	3	6	1	5	8	2
6	8	2	7	5	9	1	4	3
3	6	7	9	8	2	4	1	5
8	9	1	6	4	5	2	3	7
2	5	4	1	3	7	8	6	9
1	3	8	5	7	6	9	2	4
4	7	6	2	9	8	3	5	1
9	2	5	4	1	3	6	7	8

94

6	1	4	9	5	3	2	8	7
3	2	7	8	1	4	6	9	5
8	5	9	6	7	2	3	1	4
2	9	6	4	3	7	8	5	1
7	8	3	1	6	5	9	4	2
1	4	5	2	9	8	7	6	3
9	3	1	5	2	6	4	7	8
4	6	2	7	8	1	5	3	9
5	7	8	3	4	9	1	2	6

Solutions

95

2	6	7	5	9	4	1	3	8
9	8	3	6	1	7	4	5	2
1	5	4	2	8	3	7	6	9
4	1	5	3	6	2	9	8	7
3	7	2	8	4	9	6	1	5
8	9	6	1	7	5	3	2	4
5	2	9	4	3	6	8	7	1
6	4	1	7	5	8	2	9	3
7	3	8	9	2	1	5	4	6

96

5	2	4	8	7	3	6	9	1
8	7	6	2	1	9	3	5	4
3	1	9	5	6	4	2	7	8
7	3	2	1	9	8	4	6	5
1	4	8	7	5	6	9	2	3
6	9	5	3	4	2	1	8	7
2	6	1	4	8	7	5	3	9
9	5	7	6	3	1	8	4	2
4	8	3	9	2	5	7	1	6

Solutions

8	7	3	1	2	5	4	6	9
9	5	1	8	4	6	3	2	7
6	4	2	3	7	9	1	5	8
2	9	6	7	3	4	5	8	1
4	3	5	9	1	8	2	7	6
1	8	7	6	5	2	9	4	3
3	1	4	2	8	7	6	9	5
5	6	8	4	9	1	7	3	2
7	2	9	5	6	3	8	1	4

2	4	3	8	1	7	5	6	9
7	5	6	3	4	9	8	2	1
9	1	8	2	6	5	3	7	4
8	6	1	4	2	3	9	5	7
3	9	4	5	7	1	2	8	6
5	7	2	6	9	8	4	1	3
1	8	5	9	3	6	7	4	2
4	3	7	1	8	2	6	9	5
6	2	9	7	5	4	1	3	8

Solutions

7	2	8	3	1	5	6	9	4
3	9	6	8	4	2	1	5	7
1	4	5	7	6	9	8	2	3
9	8	4	6	5	7	3	1	2
2	6	3	4	9	1	7	8	5
5	7	1	2	3	8	4	6	9
4	5	9	1	7	6	2	3	8
8	1	7	9	2	3	5	4	6
6	3	2	5	8	4	9	7	1

5	4	8	7	9	3	1	2	6
6	3	1	2	4	8	9	7	5
2	9	7	5	6	1	8	4	3
1	2	6	3	8	5	4	9	7
9	8	3	6	7	4	5	1	2
7	5	4	1	2	9	6	3	8
8	6	2	9	1	7	3	5	4
4	1	5	8	3	2	7	6	9
3	7	9	4	5	6	2	8	1

Solutions

101

7	6	2	9	3	4	1	8	5
3	1	5	8	7	2	4	9	6
8	4	9	6	1	5	2	7	3
1	5	8	4	6	7	9	3	2
9	7	3	5	2	1	8	6	4
6	2	4	3	8	9	5	1	7
5	3	7	2	9	8	6	4	1
2	9	6	1	4	3	7	5	8
4	8	1	7	5	6	3	2	9

102

9	1	5	7	8	3	4	2	6
3	4	6	2	5	1	8	7	9
2	8	7	9	4	6	5	1	3
1	5	3	4	7	2	6	9	8
7	9	4	1	6	8	2	3	5
6	2	8	3	9	5	7	4	1
4	6	1	8	3	7	9	5	2
8	7	2	5	1	9	3	6	4
5	3	9	6	2	4	1	8	7

103

8	5	9	1	2	4	7	6	3
1	2	4	6	3	7	9	5	8
6	3	7	5	9	8	4	1	2
9	6	5	8	1	2	3	4	7
4	8	1	7	6	3	5	2	9
3	7	2	4	5	9	1	8	6
2	1	8	3	7	5	6	9	4
5	9	3	2	4	6	8	7	1
7	4	6	9	8	1	2	3	5

104

3	9	1	6	2	5	7	8	4
4	5	7	3	9	8	2	6	1
2	8	6	7	1	4	9	3	5
8	1	2	5	3	7	4	9	6
7	6	3	9	4	1	5	2	8
9	4	5	8	6	2	1	7	3
6	2	9	4	5	3	8	1	7
1	7	4	2	8	6	3	5	9
5	3	8	1	7	9	6	4	2

Solutions

105

8	3	2	4	6	7	9	5	1
6	1	5	2	9	3	4	8	7
7	4	9	1	8	5	2	6	3
1	6	4	9	3	8	7	2	5
2	9	8	7	5	1	3	4	6
3	5	7	6	2	4	8	1	9
9	7	1	8	4	6	5	3	2
5	8	6	3	7	2	1	9	4
4	2	3	5	1	9	6	7	8

106

8	5	7	4	9	2	1	3	6
3	4	1	8	5	6	7	9	2
2	9	6	7	3	1	4	5	8
9	1	3	5	8	7	2	6	4
4	2	5	6	1	9	8	7	3
6	7	8	3	2	4	5	1	9
7	3	4	1	6	8	9	2	5
5	8	9	2	7	3	6	4	1
1	6	2	9	4	5	3	8	7

Solutions

107

7	8	4	3	6	9	2	5	1
9	6	5	2	4	1	3	7	8
2	3	1	8	7	5	9	6	4
6	7	3	4	9	2	1	8	5
8	5	2	6	1	3	4	9	7
1	4	9	7	5	8	6	3	2
4	1	6	9	8	7	5	2	3
3	9	8	5	2	4	7	1	6
5	2	7	1	3	6	8	4	9

108

6	4	2	8	3	5	9	7	1
7	5	1	9	4	6	8	3	2
3	9	8	1	2	7	6	5	4
2	8	5	3	1	9	4	6	7
4	7	6	2	5	8	1	9	3
9	1	3	7	6	4	5	2	8
8	3	4	6	9	2	7	1	5
1	6	7	5	8	3	2	4	9
5	2	9	4	7	1	3	8	6

Solutions

109

1	7	5	8	6	3	4	2	9
8	6	4	7	2	9	1	5	3
9	3	2	5	1	4	6	8	7
2	1	7	6	4	8	3	9	5
5	9	3	1	7	2	8	4	6
4	8	6	3	9	5	2	7	1
7	4	9	2	3	6	5	1	8
6	5	1	4	8	7	9	3	2
3	2	8	9	5	1	7	6	4

110

3	6	8	2	5	9	1	4	7
5	2	1	8	7	4	6	9	3
9	4	7	6	1	3	5	2	8
8	3	6	9	4	7	2	5	1
2	7	9	1	8	5	3	6	4
4	1	5	3	6	2	7	8	9
6	9	2	4	3	1	8	7	5
7	8	3	5	9	6	4	1	2
1	5	4	7	2	8	9	3	6

111

5	1	3	6	2	8	4	9	7
9	7	4	3	1	5	2	6	8
8	2	6	7	4	9	1	5	3
6	3	9	8	5	4	7	2	1
1	4	8	9	7	2	6	3	5
7	5	2	1	6	3	9	8	4
3	9	7	2	8	1	5	4	6
2	6	5	4	3	7	8	1	9
4	8	1	5	9	6	3	7	2

112

4	9	8	2	7	1	3	6	5
7	5	1	8	6	3	4	2	9
2	6	3	4	9	5	8	7	1
3	1	7	9	8	4	2	5	6
6	2	9	3	5	7	1	8	4
8	4	5	6	1	2	9	3	7
9	8	4	7	2	6	5	1	3
5	7	2	1	3	9	6	4	8
1	3	6	5	4	8	7	9	2

Solutions

113

9	5	3	1	2	7	4	6	8
8	4	6	9	5	3	1	7	2
2	1	7	6	8	4	5	9	3
1	3	2	7	4	9	8	5	6
4	7	9	5	6	8	2	3	1
6	8	5	3	1	2	9	4	7
5	6	8	4	7	1	3	2	9
3	2	4	8	9	6	7	1	5
7	9	1	2	3	5	6	8	4

114

9	4	2	8	7	1	6	5	3
7	6	5	3	4	2	8	1	9
8	1	3	9	5	6	7	2	4
5	2	8	6	9	7	4	3	1
3	9	1	5	8	4	2	7	6
6	7	4	2	1	3	5	9	8
1	5	7	4	3	8	9	6	2
2	8	9	1	6	5	3	4	7
4	3	6	7	2	9	1	8	5

Solutions

115

7	1	3	4	8	2	6	5	9
6	4	8	1	5	9	2	7	3
9	5	2	7	3	6	1	4	8
3	6	9	5	4	7	8	1	2
5	7	1	3	2	8	9	6	4
2	8	4	9	6	1	7	3	5
4	2	7	6	9	3	5	8	1
8	3	6	2	1	5	4	9	7
1	9	5	8	7	4	3	2	6

116

6	9	5	7	3	2	4	1	8
4	3	2	9	1	8	5	6	7
1	8	7	4	6	5	2	9	3
9	7	1	5	2	3	8	4	6
2	6	4	8	9	7	3	5	1
8	5	3	6	4	1	9	7	2
3	1	9	2	5	6	7	8	4
7	4	6	3	8	9	1	2	5
5	2	8	1	7	4	6	3	9

Solutions

117

2	7	1	6	8	9	5	3	4
5	4	6	3	7	2	8	9	1
3	9	8	4	5	1	2	6	7
1	5	3	7	9	8	4	2	6
8	2	9	1	6	4	7	5	3
7	6	4	2	3	5	9	1	8
4	8	2	9	1	3	6	7	5
6	3	5	8	2	7	1	4	9
9	1	7	5	4	6	3	8	2

118

3	1	7	9	6	2	8	5	4
2	4	9	7	5	8	1	3	6
8	6	5	4	1	3	2	9	7
1	9	6	3	8	5	4	7	2
4	2	8	1	9	7	3	6	5
5	7	3	6	2	4	9	8	1
6	5	2	8	4	9	7	1	3
7	8	4	5	3	1	6	2	9
9	3	1	2	7	6	5	4	8

Solutions

119

3	6	5	7	8	9	2	1	4
2	9	1	4	5	3	7	6	8
4	7	8	1	6	2	5	9	3
8	2	7	9	4	5	1	3	6
9	1	4	2	3	6	8	7	5
6	5	3	8	1	7	9	4	2
7	3	6	5	9	8	4	2	1
5	4	2	3	7	1	6	8	9
1	8	9	6	2	4	3	5	7

120

4	8	2	9	5	6	1	3	7
7	5	1	3	8	4	9	2	6
6	9	3	7	1	2	8	5	4
5	1	9	6	2	8	4	7	3
8	3	6	4	7	9	2	1	5
2	7	4	1	3	5	6	8	9
1	6	8	5	9	3	7	4	2
3	4	7	2	6	1	5	9	8
9	2	5	8	4	7	3	6	1

Solutions

121

5	8	4	7	6	1	9	2	3
3	7	1	9	4	2	5	6	8
2	6	9	3	5	8	1	7	4
9	2	3	6	1	7	8	4	5
6	4	5	2	8	3	7	9	1
8	1	7	5	9	4	2	3	6
4	9	6	8	7	5	3	1	2
7	3	8	1	2	6	4	5	9
1	5	2	4	3	9	6	8	7

122

5	9	6	4	7	3	1	8	2
4	8	2	1	9	5	6	7	3
7	3	1	2	6	8	5	4	9
6	5	4	3	2	9	8	1	7
1	2	9	7	8	4	3	6	5
8	7	3	5	1	6	2	9	4
9	6	7	8	5	2	4	3	1
3	1	5	6	4	7	9	2	8
2	4	8	9	3	1	7	5	6

Solutions

123

8	9	7	3	2	1	6	4	5
3	5	1	4	7	6	9	2	8
4	2	6	5	8	9	3	1	7
7	3	4	9	5	2	8	6	1
6	1	9	7	3	8	4	5	2
2	8	5	1	6	4	7	9	3
5	6	3	2	4	7	1	8	9
1	4	2	8	9	3	5	7	6
9	7	8	6	1	5	2	3	4

124

1	4	7	9	8	3	5	6	2
2	9	5	6	1	7	4	8	3
8	6	3	4	2	5	9	1	7
4	3	1	8	7	6	2	5	9
5	8	6	3	9	2	1	7	4
7	2	9	5	4	1	6	3	8
3	1	8	2	6	4	7	9	5
6	5	2	7	3	9	8	4	1
9	7	4	1	5	8	3	2	6

Solutions

125

1	4	8	7	2	9	5	6	3
3	6	7	5	8	4	1	2	9
9	2	5	3	6	1	8	4	7
5	8	9	2	1	7	6	3	4
4	3	1	6	9	5	2	7	8
6	7	2	8	4	3	9	5	1
8	9	3	4	5	2	7	1	6
2	1	4	9	7	6	3	8	5
7	5	6	1	3	8	4	9	2

126

8	1	5	9	6	2	3	4	7
6	3	7	5	1	4	2	8	9
9	4	2	3	8	7	5	1	6
7	2	9	8	3	6	4	5	1
3	5	8	4	9	1	6	7	2
4	6	1	7	2	5	9	3	8
5	9	6	1	4	8	7	2	3
1	7	3	2	5	9	8	6	4
2	8	4	6	7	3	1	9	5

127

4	3	5	9	1	8	7	6	2
2	6	1	7	4	3	9	8	5
8	7	9	6	2	5	3	1	4
1	5	6	2	8	9	4	3	7
9	4	2	1	3	7	6	5	8
7	8	3	5	6	4	2	9	1
5	2	8	3	7	6	1	4	9
3	9	7	4	5	1	8	2	6
6	1	4	8	9	2	5	7	3

128

7	8	9	4	2	6	5	1	3
2	4	6	1	5	3	8	7	9
5	3	1	9	8	7	6	2	4
4	2	3	5	1	8	7	9	6
8	1	5	6	7	9	4	3	2
9	6	7	3	4	2	1	5	8
1	9	2	8	6	5	3	4	7
6	7	4	2	3	1	9	8	5
3	5	8	7	9	4	2	6	1

Solutions

129

9	2	5	7	1	3	4	6	8
1	7	6	4	2	8	9	3	5
4	3	8	5	9	6	2	7	1
3	5	9	8	4	7	1	2	6
2	1	4	3	6	9	5	8	7
8	6	7	2	5	1	3	9	4
7	8	2	1	3	5	6	4	9
5	9	3	6	8	4	7	1	2
6	4	1	9	7	2	8	5	3

130

2	5	1	7	4	8	6	3	9
7	6	8	5	9	3	4	1	2
9	3	4	6	2	1	7	8	5
3	2	9	8	5	6	1	7	4
4	8	5	1	7	2	9	6	3
6	1	7	9	3	4	5	2	8
5	4	6	3	8	7	2	9	1
1	9	3	2	6	5	8	4	7
8	7	2	4	1	9	3	5	6

Solutions

131

5	2	9	7	6	1	4	3	8
8	7	4	9	5	3	2	6	1
1	3	6	8	2	4	9	7	5
9	8	1	2	7	5	3	4	6
3	5	2	6	4	9	8	1	7
4	6	7	3	1	8	5	2	9
2	9	5	1	3	6	7	8	4
7	1	8	4	9	2	6	5	3
6	4	3	5	8	7	1	9	2

132

9	6	7	1	4	5	2	3	8
4	1	8	3	2	9	7	5	6
5	3	2	6	8	7	4	1	9
7	8	4	9	5	1	3	6	2
3	5	9	4	6	2	8	7	1
6	2	1	7	3	8	9	4	5
1	4	3	2	9	6	5	8	7
8	9	6	5	7	3	1	2	4
2	7	5	8	1	4	6	9	3

Solutions

133

5	8	3	4	1	7	2	9	6
4	1	6	5	9	2	3	7	8
2	9	7	6	8	3	5	4	1
3	4	2	7	6	8	1	5	9
1	6	9	3	5	4	8	2	7
7	5	8	1	2	9	6	3	4
6	2	5	9	7	1	4	8	3
9	3	1	8	4	5	7	6	2
8	7	4	2	3	6	9	1	5

134

5	3	7	4	2	8	9	6	1
2	1	8	6	7	9	4	3	5
9	6	4	1	5	3	2	7	8
6	8	1	5	3	4	7	2	9
4	9	2	7	8	1	3	5	6
7	5	3	9	6	2	1	8	4
3	7	9	8	1	6	5	4	2
1	2	6	3	4	5	8	9	7
8	4	5	2	9	7	6	1	3

135

6	1	7	8	4	9	2	5	3
8	5	9	3	7	2	1	6	4
4	3	2	6	1	5	8	7	9
5	8	3	7	6	1	4	9	2
9	2	1	4	5	3	6	8	7
7	4	6	9	2	8	5	3	1
2	9	5	1	3	6	7	4	8
1	7	8	5	9	4	3	2	6
3	6	4	2	8	7	9	1	5

136

6	3	7	2	9	5	8	4	1
1	9	2	6	4	8	7	3	5
8	5	4	7	3	1	6	9	2
5	4	9	1	6	2	3	7	8
2	1	8	4	7	3	9	5	6
3	7	6	8	5	9	2	1	4
4	2	1	3	8	7	5	6	9
9	8	3	5	1	6	4	2	7
7	6	5	9	2	4	1	8	3

Solutions

137

8	3	6	5	2	9	4	1	7
1	7	9	8	4	6	5	3	2
2	5	4	7	3	1	9	6	8
4	9	3	2	7	8	6	5	1
7	2	5	1	6	4	8	9	3
6	1	8	3	9	5	7	2	4
5	6	1	4	8	2	3	7	9
3	8	2	9	5	7	1	4	6
9	4	7	6	1	3	2	8	5

138

2	6	5	7	1	8	9	4	3
9	3	7	4	2	5	1	8	6
8	4	1	3	9	6	5	2	7
5	2	6	1	4	3	7	9	8
1	7	8	5	6	9	2	3	4
4	9	3	2	8	7	6	5	1
6	1	4	9	3	2	8	7	5
7	8	2	6	5	4	3	1	9
3	5	9	8	7	1	4	6	2

Solutions

139

8	5	6	3	2	4	7	9	1
9	7	2	1	5	8	6	3	4
1	4	3	9	7	6	8	2	5
6	8	1	7	3	9	5	4	2
2	9	7	8	4	5	3	1	6
5	3	4	2	6	1	9	7	8
3	2	5	4	8	7	1	6	9
7	6	9	5	1	2	4	8	3
4	1	8	6	9	3	2	5	7

140

5	3	7	4	2	1	8	9	6
1	8	6	7	5	9	2	3	4
4	9	2	3	6	8	7	5	1
6	7	5	1	8	2	9	4	3
9	1	4	5	3	7	6	8	2
8	2	3	9	4	6	1	7	5
3	6	8	2	7	4	5	1	9
2	5	9	8	1	3	4	6	7
7	4	1	6	9	5	3	2	8

Solutions

141

4	3	1	6	9	7	2	5	8
9	8	5	4	3	2	1	6	7
6	2	7	5	1	8	3	9	4
5	9	3	2	4	6	7	8	1
7	1	6	3	8	5	4	2	9
8	4	2	9	7	1	6	3	5
2	5	8	1	6	4	9	7	3
1	6	9	7	5	3	8	4	2
3	7	4	8	2	9	5	1	6

142

9	6	2	3	4	5	1	8	7
5	7	1	2	9	8	3	6	4
8	4	3	7	1	6	5	9	2
4	8	5	9	6	3	7	2	1
3	9	6	1	2	7	8	4	5
2	1	7	5	8	4	6	3	9
6	3	9	4	7	1	2	5	8
7	2	8	6	5	9	4	1	3
1	5	4	8	3	2	9	7	6

143

7	8	3	5	4	6	1	2	9
9	2	6	8	7	1	3	4	5
1	4	5	9	3	2	7	6	8
6	7	8	4	2	9	5	1	3
4	5	9	6	1	3	8	7	2
3	1	2	7	8	5	6	9	4
5	3	1	2	6	4	9	8	7
2	9	7	1	5	8	4	3	6
8	6	4	3	9	7	2	5	1

144

8	4	2	9	7	6	5	1	3
9	5	1	3	8	2	4	6	7
3	7	6	5	4	1	2	8	9
4	6	3	1	9	5	8	7	2
2	8	9	7	6	4	1	3	5
5	1	7	8	2	3	6	9	4
6	9	4	2	1	7	3	5	8
7	2	5	6	3	8	9	4	1
1	3	8	4	5	9	7	2	6

Solutions

9	1	3	6	8	2	4	7	5
4	7	6	3	9	5	2	1	8
2	8	5	7	1	4	6	3	9
3	4	7	5	2	6	8	9	1
6	9	1	8	7	3	5	2	4
5	2	8	9	4	1	7	6	3
8	6	4	1	3	7	9	5	2
1	5	9	2	6	8	3	4	7
7	3	2	4	5	9	1	8	6

8	5	1	6	9	3	2	7	4
6	2	7	4	1	8	3	9	5
3	9	4	7	5	2	6	8	1
4	1	2	8	6	9	7	5	3
7	3	9	1	2	5	4	6	8
5	8	6	3	7	4	9	1	2
1	7	5	2	4	6	8	3	9
9	4	3	5	8	7	1	2	6
2	6	8	9	3	1	5	4	7

Solutions

147

4	3	6	9	1	2	8	7	5
7	2	9	5	4	8	3	1	6
1	5	8	3	6	7	9	4	2
2	4	7	8	3	9	6	5	1
8	6	3	7	5	1	2	9	4
9	1	5	6	2	4	7	3	8
6	8	4	1	7	3	5	2	9
3	9	1	2	8	5	4	6	7
5	7	2	4	9	6	1	8	3

148

8	6	7	2	3	1	4	9	5
5	9	4	6	8	7	2	3	1
3	1	2	9	4	5	6	8	7
7	8	6	1	5	2	3	4	9
2	3	1	7	9	4	8	5	6
4	5	9	8	6	3	7	1	2
6	7	3	4	1	9	5	2	8
1	4	8	5	2	6	9	7	3
9	2	5	3	7	8	1	6	4

Solutions

3	5	2	8	9	6	7	1	4
4	1	8	7	2	5	9	3	6
9	6	7	4	1	3	5	8	2
1	7	5	3	6	2	4	9	8
2	9	6	1	8	4	3	7	5
8	3	4	9	5	7	2	6	1
5	8	3	2	7	1	6	4	9
7	2	1	6	4	9	8	5	3
6	4	9	5	3	8	1	2	7

5	1	6	2	3	7	8	9	4
2	4	9	5	8	1	3	6	7
3	8	7	6	4	9	1	5	2
7	9	8	1	5	2	4	3	6
6	3	1	9	7	4	5	2	8
4	2	5	3	6	8	9	7	1
1	6	2	4	9	3	7	8	5
8	5	3	7	1	6	2	4	9
9	7	4	8	2	5	6	1	3

Solutions